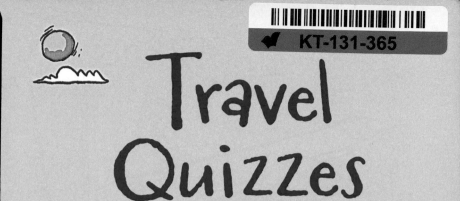

Travel
Quizzes

Simon Tudhope and Kirsteen Robson

Illustrated by Sarah Horne

Designed by Kate Rimmer

Edited by Sam Smith
and Sam Taplin

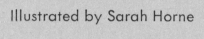

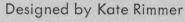

5 On a trek through the rainforest, which of these animals would you never come across?

a) poison-dart frog
b) naked mole rat
c) blood-sucking leech ✓

✗

6 What's opposite to northwest? Southwest ✗

7 If you saw a snake charmer in India, would he be using a real snake? No ✗

8 What type of boat is this man paddling through the canals of Venice?

Gondola

3/8

1. Who built the Acropolis?

   a) Romans   b) Saxons   c) Ancient Greeks ✓

2. 'Ships of the desert' are...

   a) camels ✓   b) jeeps   c) hovercraft

3. One fifth of all the people in the world are Chinese.
   True or false?   *True*

4. In 1912, why did the first woman to fly across the
   English Channel get so little attention from the media?

   a) it was frowned upon for women to fly
   b) the *Titanic* had sunk the day before
   c) no one believed her

   b) The Titanic sunk the day before ✓

5. Which character flew from England
   to America in a giant peach carried
   by seagulls?

   a) Charlie
   b) James ✓ ✓
   c) Matilda

6 Which mythical creatures were said to lure sailors to their doom?

a) banshees ✓   b) sirens ✗   c) harpies

7 Which is the only one of the seven continents that doesn't have a desert?

a) Europe ✓   b) Asia   c) North America

8 New Orleans, the jazz capital of America, is also known as the 'Big...?'

a) Apple   b) Sleep ✗   c) Easy ✓

9 Where would you find the Sea of Tranquility?

a) underneath the Antarctic ice sheet

b) off the coast of Australia

c) on the Moon ✓

10 Which volcano erupted near the Roman town of Pompeii, burying it under a thick blanket of ash?

a) Popocatépetl

b) Mount Vesuvius ✓

c) Mount Etna

11 What nickname do sailors traditionally use for the bottom of the sea: The Captain's Graveyard or Davy Jones's Locker?

The Captain's Graveyard ✗

9/11

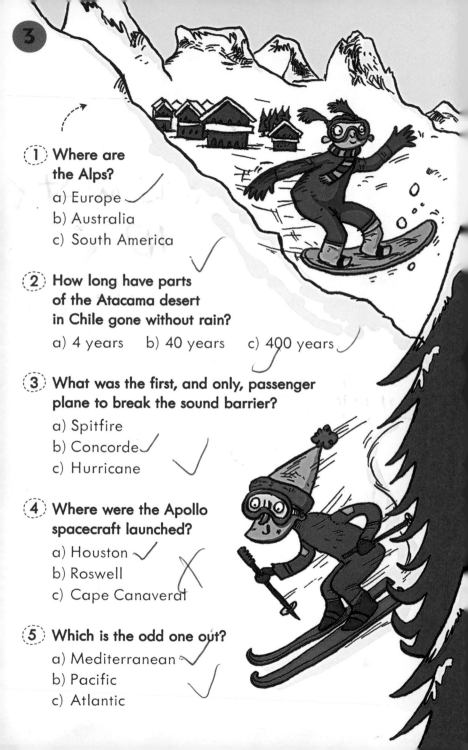

3

1 Where are
the Alps?

a) Europe
b) Australia
c) South America

2 How long have parts
of the Atacama desert
in Chile gone without rain?

a) 4 years   b) 40 years   c) 400 years

3 What was the first, and only, passenger
plane to break the sound barrier?

a) Spitfire
b) Concorde
c) Hurricane

4 Where were the Apollo
spacecraft launched?

a) Houston
b) Roswell
c) Cape Canaveral

5 Which is the odd one out?

a) Mediterranean
b) Pacific
c) Atlantic

6 What is Peru's capital city?

a) Tunis   b) Kingston   c) Lima ✓

7 Which character has a blue box that can travel through time and space?

a) Doctor Who ✓
b) Captain Kirk
c) Darth Vader

8 Where is St. Basil's cathedral?

a) Finland
b) Russia ✓
c) Scotland

9 How many people are there in the world?

a) 7 billion
b) 10 billion ✓
c) 13 billion

10 Which is NOT a real place?

a) Transylvania ✓   b) Zanzibar   c) Valhalla

7/10

4

1. Which brothers made the first hot-air balloon, over 100 years before planes were invented?
   a) Montgolfier
   b) Grimm
   c) Jackson ✓

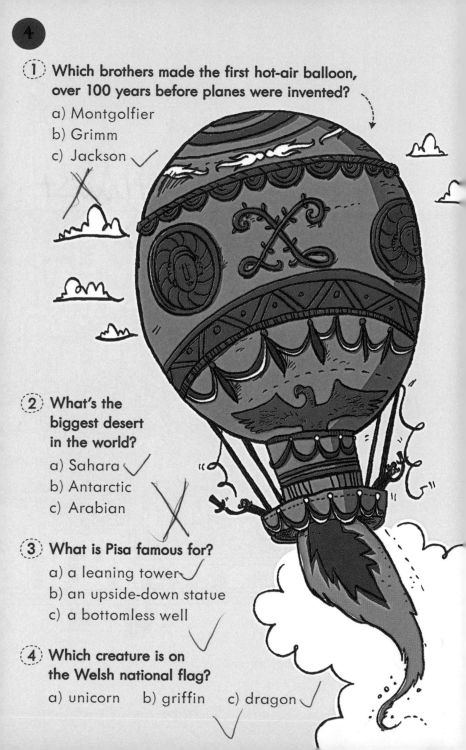

2. What's the biggest desert in the world?
   a) Sahara ✓
   b) Antarctic
   c) Arabian ✗

3. What is Pisa famous for?
   a) a leaning tower ✓
   b) an upside-down statue
   c) a bottomless well ✓

4. Which creature is on the Welsh national flag?
   a) unicorn   b) griffin   c) dragon ✓

5 Where could you stay in a hotel made of ice?

   a) Sweden ✓ b) Jordan c) Malaysia
   ✓

6 Which country has a wheel in the middle of its flag?

   a) India ✓
   b) Cuba ✓
   c) Japan ✓

7 How are the Royal Canadian mounted police better known?

   The Mounties ✓

8 Where's Mount Everest?

   a) India
   b) Burma
   c) Nepal ✓ ✓

9 Where's Lake Baikal, the world's deepest lake?

   a) Norway
   b) Russia ✗
   c) Iceland ✓

6/9

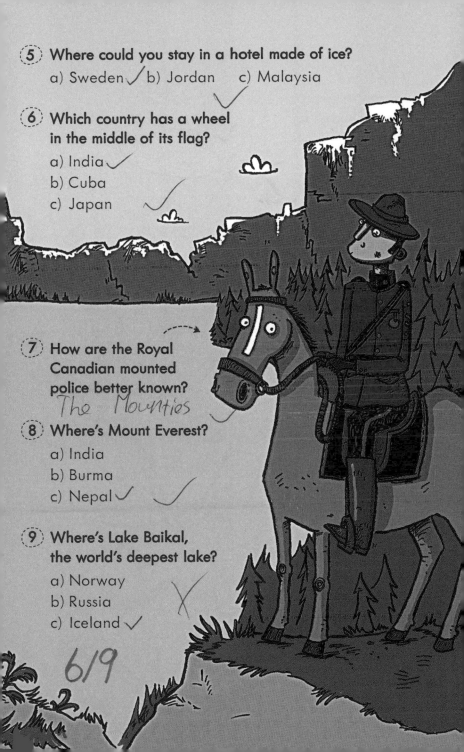

5

1) Where can you see religious dancers known as 'whirling dervishes'?
   a) Mexico
   b) Turkey
   c) Russia

2) Where is Mount Olympus?
   a) Greece   b) Italy   c) Bulgaria

3) Which language is spoken by the most people?
   a) Arabic
   b) English
   c) Chinese

4) Which is the odd one out?
   a) Brazil
   b) Tokyo
   c) Sweden

5) Where are Marrakech and Casablanca?
   a) Morocco
   b) Sudan
   c) Chad

6 Where can you see the Shaolin Monastery, where some of the world's best martial artists are trained?

a) Thailand

b) China

c) Japan ✗

7 Put these countries in order from north to south.

a) Mongolia 2

b) Norway 1

c) Fiji 3

8 Roughly what speed does the Earth travel around the Sun?

a) 10,000km/h / 6,000mph

b) 100,000km/h / 60,000mph

c) 1,000,000km/h / 600,000mph

9 Which part of a ship is the bow: front or back?

7/9

6

1. Can a passenger plane survive being struck by lightning? Yes ✓

2. On safari, when are you most likely to see animals drinking at a waterhole: the middle of the day or dawn and dusk? ✓

3. Which civilization built pyramids in the rainforests of Central America?
   a) Celts   b) Apaches   c) Mayans ✓

4. Where are the Himalayas?
   a) Asia ✓
   b) Africa
   c) Oceania

5. Waffles and maple syrup are a traditional food in which country?
   a) Canada ✓
   b) Philippines
   c) Germany

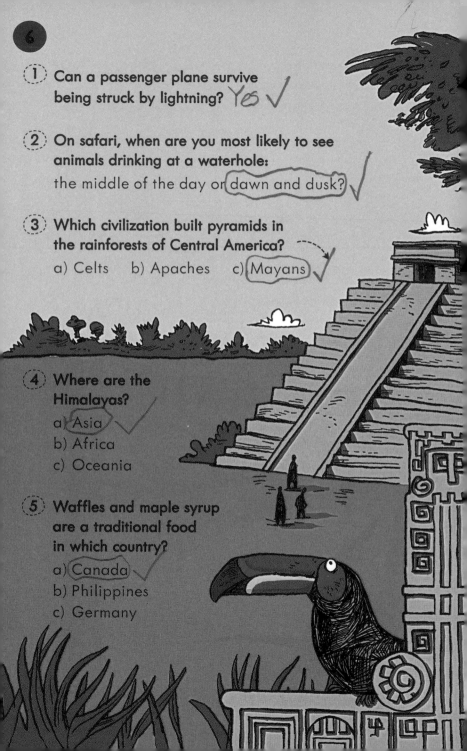

6 Which is the highest mountain in the world?

a) Kilimanjaro
b) Everest ✓
c) K2

7 What does the Spanish word "gringo" mean?

a) foreigner ✓
b) fisherman
c) friend

8 Which is the largest country in South America?

a) Argentina
b) Ecuador
c) Brazil ✓

9 What is New Zealand's capital city?

a) Johannesburg
b) Melbourne
c) Wellington ✓

9/9

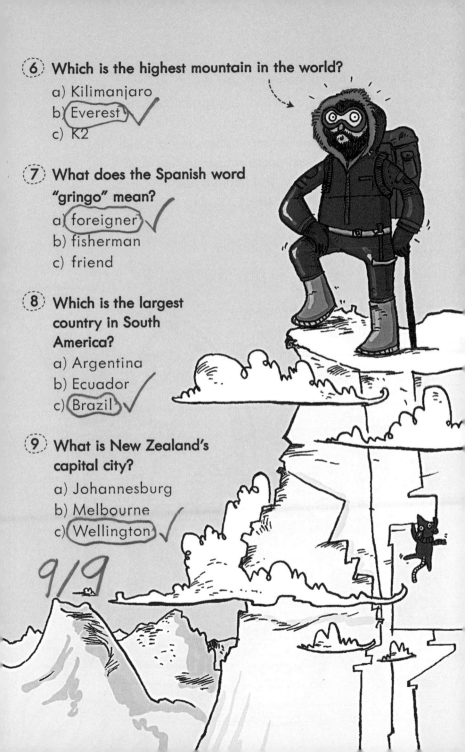

1. In bullfights, do matadors use a...
   a) black cape?   b) blue cape?   c) red cape?

2. Which word goes before 'snowman' to make the nickname of the mythical half-man half-ape creature that lives in the Himalayas?
   a) Abominable   b) Despicable   c) Abysmal

3. Which is the largest country in Africa?
   a) South Africa   b) Madagascar   c) Algeria

4. What hats are this Mexican mariachi band wearing?
   a) stetsons
   b) sombreros
   c) tam o'shanters

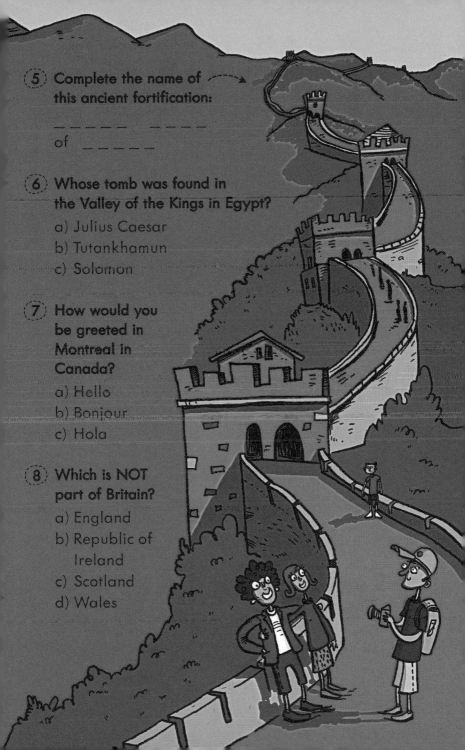

(5) Complete the name of
this ancient fortification:

_ _ _ _ _   _ _ _ _

of _ _ _ _ _

(6) Whose tomb was found in
the Valley of the Kings in Egypt?

a) Julius Caesar
b) Tutankhamun
c) Solomon

(7) How would you
be greeted in
Montreal in
Canada?

a) Hello
b) Bonjour
c) Hola

(8) Which is NOT
part of Britain?

a) England
b) Republic of
Ireland
c) Scotland
d) Wales

8

1. Was the city of Troy in modern-day Greece or Turkey?

2. What's the traditional robe that's worn in Japan on special occasions?
   a) kimono   b) toga   c) kaftan

3. If you sneezed in Germany, what would somebody say?
   a) Schnitzel!
   b) Lederhosen!
   c) Gesundheit!

4. Which travels faster: light or sound?

5. The largest continent is...
   a) North America
   b) Africa
   c) Asia

6 Which is older:
the Eiffel Tower or the Statue of Liberty?

7 The world's
largest ocean is...
a) Atlantic
b) Pacific
c) Indian

8 Which character was shipwrecked on a Caribbean island?
a) Robinson Crusoe   b) Don Quixote   c) Gulliver

9 Sand on white beaches is NOT made from ground up...
a) fish bones   b) coral   c) shells

1. Only one of the Poles has land beneath it. Which is it: North or South?

2. I was the largest and most luxurious ship ever built. They called me 'unsinkable'...
   ...but I was sunk by an iceberg on my first voyage.
   What am I?

3. Which Italian city is the birthplace of pizza?
   a) Milan
   b) Naples
   c) Pisa

4. Which snake might you see in the desert?
   a) sidewinding adder
   b) boa constrictor
   c) green mamba

5. If you step eastward across the international date line, do you go back one day or forward one day?

(6) What's the name of the curtains of light that billow over Scandinavia's far north?

(7) Is more of the Earth covered by sea or land?

(8) Which English seaside town is famous for its fish and chips, and for being terrorized by Dracula in the book by Bram Stoker?
a) Brighton
b) Blackpool
c) Whitby

(9) Which animal can you see in Kenya?
a) wolf
b) wombat
c) warthog

1 Which ocean is between South America and Africa?

a) Atlantic   b) Arctic   c) Pacific

2 Pilots measure the speed of their plane in...

a) light years   b) knots   c) air miles

3 Where are the
Rocky Mountains?

a) Europe

b) Oceania

c) North America

4 If you traced around a map of Italy's
coastline, what would your picture look like?

a) a boot   b) a T-shirt   c) a bow tie

5 Which capital city is furthest south?

    a) Berlin   b) Helsinki   c) Mogadishu

6 Which type of bear does NOT live in Canada?

    a) grizzly bear   b) panda   c) polar bear

7 What are the summer storms that provide 80% of India's yearly rainfall?

    a) monsoons   b) typhoons   c) cyclones

8 What traditional Russian instrument looks like a triangular guitar?

    a) mandolin
    b) balalaika
    c) hurdy gurdy

1 Is sleeping in an igloo like sleeping in a:

a) supermarket freezer?
b) walk-in fridge?
c) warm oven?

2 I have two big orange teeth...
...and a talent for felling trees.
I'm also Canada's national animal.
What am I?

3 Which dogs pull snow sleds?

a) huskies
b) Dalmatians
c) bloodhounds

4 On a daytime flight, is it always sunny above the clouds?

5 Which of these rivers is longest?

    a) Amazon   b) Congo   c) Yangtze

6 Which city do the most jumbo jets land in each year?

    a) New York   b) Beijing   c) London

7 I turn red at dawn and dusk, and weigh 4 million tons. One of my names is 'Uluru'.

    What's my other name?

8 Which country is home of the didgeridoo?

    a) Australia

    b) Kenya

    c) Brazil

1 In Uzbekistan there's a city in the desert called Samarkand. Which trade route made it one of the richest cities in the world?

a) Silk Road
b) Cotton Road
c) Nylon Road

2 When comparing the size of one country to another, which is more accurate: a globe or a flat map?

3 Which country's national animal is the bald eagle?

a) Egypt   b) Italy   c) United States

4 What do people traditionally eat with in China?

a) knife and fork   b) chopsticks   c) their fingers

5) Who was the first person to fly solo across the Atlantic?
   a) Charles Lindbergh
   b) Neil Armstrong
   c) James Cook

6) What's the nickname for Japan's high-speed trains?
   a) bullet trains   b) rocket trains   c) lightning trains

7) Which side of a ship is 'starboard', left or right?

8) Where do fishermen use trained birds to catch fish?
   a) Uzbekistan   b) Ethiopia   c) China

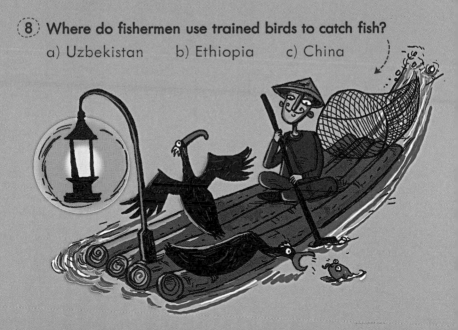

1 Which big cat might you see in the Amazon rainforest?

a) tiger   b) lion   c) jaguar

2 This church was begun by Antoni Gaudí in 1882, and is still being built. Where is it?

a) Manchester   b) Barcelona   c) Dublin

3 Modern passenger jets can fly all the way around the world without stopping.

True or false?

4 Why did Death Valley get its name?

a) it's extremely hot
b) it's extremely cold
c) it has lots of tornadoes

5 What's the capital city of Greece?

a) Olympus
b) Athens
c) Troy

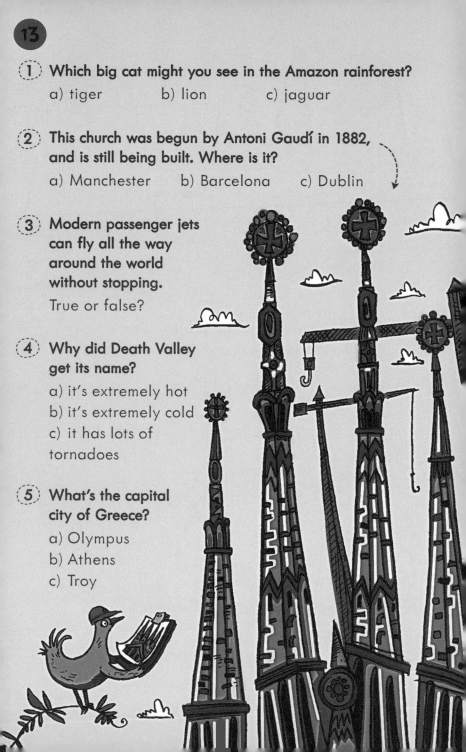

6 Match the word for 'roller coaster' with the name of the language it's written in.

a) 雲霄飛車   1) Arabic
b) ジェットコースター 2) Chinese
c) أفعوانية   3) Japanese

7 Is Hollywood on the East or West Coast of America?

8 Which area in the Atlantic Ocean have ships sailed into and never been seen again?

a) The Jamaica Circle
b) The Bermuda Triangle
c) The Haiti Square

9 Did Native Americans travel in:

a) yachts?
b) canoes?
c) dinghies?

1 **What's the Ring of Fire?**
a) a ring of volcanoes around the Pacific Ocean
b) a river of lava that corkscrews down Mount Etna
c) a roller coaster at Disneyland Florida

2 **Whose dead body has been on display in Moscow's Red Square since 1924?**
a) Karl Marx   b) Vladimir Lenin   c) Josef Stalin

3 **Which two countries are linked by the Channel Tunnel?**

4 **Which city is famous for its yellow cabs?**

5 Where can you see kangaroos in the wild?

   a) Spain   b) India   c) Australia

6 Where is Beijing the capital city?

   a) China   b) Madagascar   c) Pakistan

7 How long is the Equator?

   a) 400,000km / 250,000 miles

   b) 40,000km / 25,000 miles

   c) 4,000km / 2,500 miles

8 In India you can
be taken around
town in one of
these vehicles.
What are
they called?

   a) pedalos

   b) rickshaws

   c) gondolas

15

1 Which city at
night is this?
a) Mumbai
b) Vienna
c) Tokyo

2 Where does paella come from?
a) Spain   b) Mexico   c) France

3 Baseball is Canada's
most popular sport.
True or false?

4 The remains of which ancient
city are found in Iraq?
a) Troy
b) Atlantis
c) Babylon

5 Where's the Empire
State Building?
a) Madrid
b) New York
c) Toronto

6 Which animal could you NOT see in the wild in Africa?

a) crocodile   b) giraffe   c) tiger   d) lion

7 Where can you spend yuan?

a) Nigeria   b) Indonesia   c) China

8 Complete the name of the largest river in North America.

_ i _ _ i _ _ i _ _ i

9 Who's said to live in a snowy place called Lapland, in the Arctic Circle?

a) Santa Claus
b) the Grinch
c) the Abominable Snowman

10 Moroccan stews are cooked and served in an earthenware pot called a:

a) wok
b) tagine
c) balti

1. Would you ever see a Tasmanian devil in Tasmania?

2. Where does the pilot of a jumbo jet sit?
   a) cabin　　　b) hold　　　c) cockpit

3. How do you say 'goodbye' in Japanese?
   a) konnichiwa　　b) sayonara　　c) saru

4. Which tribe travel and trade across the Sahara desert?
   a) Sioux
   b) Bedouin
   c) Cossacks

5 Which of these is NOT a real river?

a) Blue Nile   b) Green Nile   c) White Nile

6 If a sailor was left stranded on a desert island, they would say they had been what?

a) capsized   b) marooned   c) scuttled

7 What is a bathyscaphe: a high-altitude weather balloon or a deep-sea submersible?

8 Washington D.C. in the USA is NOT a part of any state. True or false?

9 What happened in the Sahara desert in 1979?

a) a meteorite strike
b) a huge earthquake
c) it snowed

10 A 'twister' is a slang name for which type of natural phenomenon?

a) whirlpool   b) tornado   c) hurricane

1. **Who was the first woman to fly solo across the Atlantic Ocean?**
   a) Amelia Earhart
   b) Eleanor Roosevelt
   c) Katharine Hepburn

2. **Where is it rude to show someone the sole of your shoe?**
   a) North America   b) Middle East   c) Oceania

3. **Canada has two official languages. One is English. What's the other?**
   a) Spanish   b) Swedish   c) French

4. **What ships did Vikings sail in?**
   a) frigates   b) longboats   c) kayaks

5 Where was the *Titanic* sailing to when it hit an iceberg and sank?

a) New York
b) Liverpool
c) Cape Town

6 What's the largest lake in South America?

a) Titicaca
b) Titihaha
c) Tititata

7 Which mountain was said to be the home of the Greek gods:

Mount Olympus or Mount Sinai?

8 What pulls Santa's sleigh?

a) horses
b) reindeer
c) oxen

1. If you see an oasis in the desert that disappears as you walk toward it, what have you actually seen?

   m _ _ _ _ _

2. Who built the Colosseum?
   a) Egyptians
   b) Mongols
   c) Romans

3. What is Germany's capital city?
   a) Hamburg   b) Munich   c) Berlin

4. What's most likely to be on the menu in Argentina?
   a) steak
   b) caviar
   c) mock turtle soup

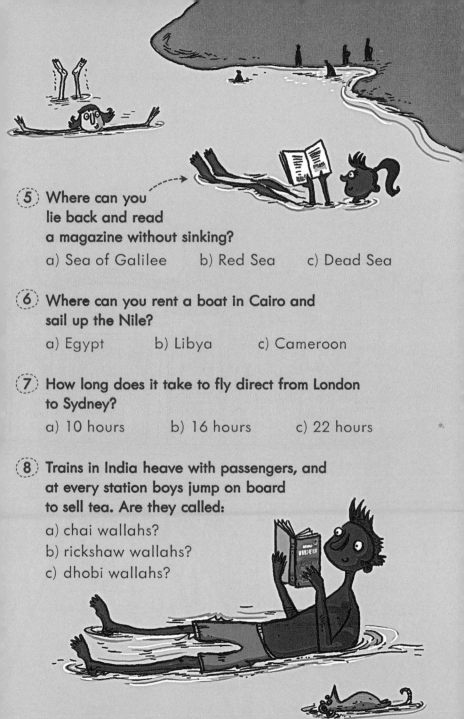

5 Where can you lie back and read a magazine without sinking?

a) Sea of Galilee   b) Red Sea   c) Dead Sea

6 Where can you rent a boat in Cairo and sail up the Nile?

a) Egypt   b) Libya   c) Cameroon

7 How long does it take to fly direct from London to Sydney?

a) 10 hours   b) 16 hours   c) 22 hours

8 Trains in India heave with passengers, and at every station boys jump on board to sell tea. Are they called:

a) chai wallahs?
b) rickshaw wallahs?
c) dhobi wallahs?

1 Where are the highest sea cliffs in the world, as tall as a 275-floor building?

    a) Hawaii   b) Iceland   c) Greece

2 Name five of the seven continents.

3 Where's the Taj Mahal?

    a) India   b) China   c) Iran

4 How many stars are there on the American flag?

    a) 5
    b) 20
    c) 50

5 Who was the first person in space?

   a) Neil Armstrong
   b) Yuri Gagarin
   c) James T Kirk

6 Which ocean would you cross if you set out from New Zealand and sailed to Peru?

   a) Pacific Ocean
   b) Atlantic Ocean
   c) Indian Ocean

7 Where are the Andes mountains?

   a) Asia   b) Europe   c) South America

8 What is Spain's capital city?

   a) Seville   b) Madrid   c) Barcelona

1 **Does the leading rider in the Tour de France cycle race wear a...**

a) red jersey?   b) yellow jersey?   c) blue jersey?

2 **Which country has a white flag with a red circle in the middle?**

a) Canada   b) Japan   c) Turkey

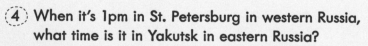

3 **On average, which pole is colder:**

the North Pole or the South Pole?

4 **When it's 1pm in St. Petersburg in western Russia, what time is it in Yakutsk in eastern Russia?**

a) 1pm   b) 5pm   c) 9pm

5 Which tribes are native to New Zealand?

a) Zulu   b) Maori   c) Apache

6 What language do people speak in Brazil?

a) French   b) Spanish   c) Portuguese

7 Where's the Great Sandy Desert?

a) United States
b) Argentina
c) Australia

8 Where are these floating markets held?

a) Ecuador
b) Thailand
c) Sudan

1) **Which line is from the chorus of Canada's national anthem?**

   a) O Canada, your land is wild and free.
   b) O Canada, we stand on guard for thee.
   c) O Canada, we love your maple trees.

2) **Which people from Ukraine and southern Russia perform this dance?**

   a) Magyars
   b) Tartars
   c) Cossacks

3) **What's the main obstacle to taking photos in Antarctica in mid-winter?**

   a) it's too cold
   b) there's no light
   c) it angers penguins

4) **Is Japan closer to the North Pole or the South Pole?**

5 Roughly how many countries are there in the world?

   a) 100   b) 200   c) 300

6 Which ship was found abandoned and drifting in the ocean, with no sign of damage and no sign of her crew?

   a) *Mary Celeste*
   b) *Victory*
   c) *Santa María*

7 Put these vehicles in the order they were invented.

   a) motorcycle   b) train   c) plane

8 These ancient statues are on which island in the Pacific Ocean?

   a) Easter Island
   b) Christmas Island
   c) Valentine Island

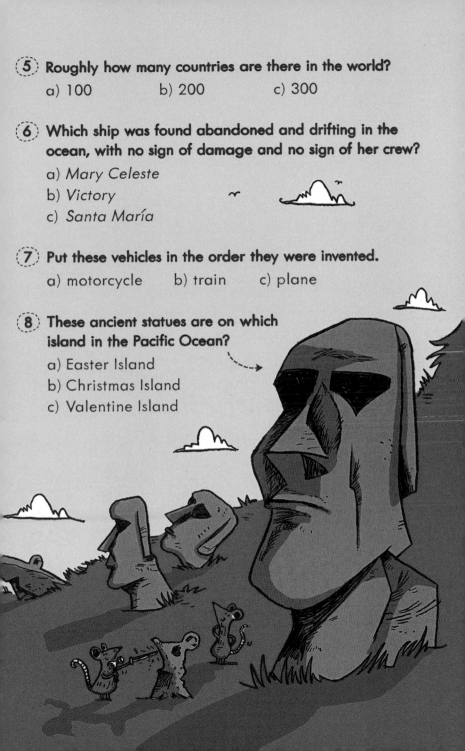

1. In Spain, a worried-looking man cries:
"¡mi toro se ha escapado!" What's he saying?
"My watch has been stolen!" or "My bull has escaped!"

2. Which of these countries is NOT in Africa?
a) Zimbabwe   b) Guatemala   c) Somalia

3. What is Santa Claus's name in Russia:
Papa Midnight or Grandfather Frost?

4. Norway's coast has thousands of narrow,
steep-sided inlets. What are they called?
a) estuaries   b) reservoirs   c) fjords

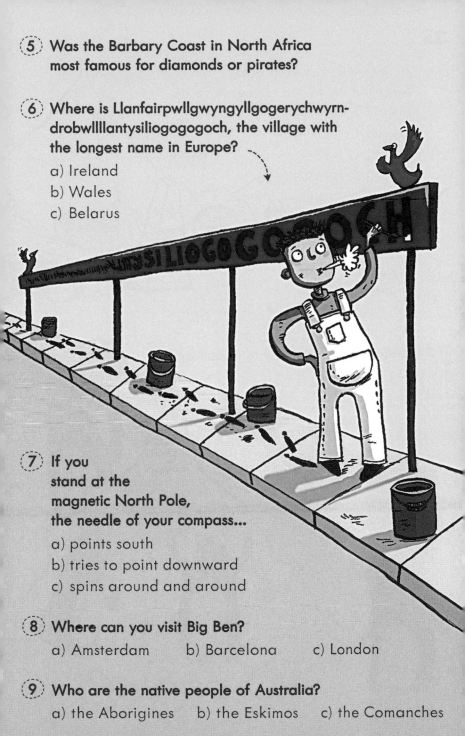

5 Was the Barbary Coast in North Africa most famous for diamonds or pirates?

6 Where is Llanfairpwllgwyngyllgogerychwyrn-drobwllllantysiliogogogoch, the village with the longest name in Europe?
a) Ireland
b) Wales
c) Belarus

7 If you stand at the magnetic North Pole, the needle of your compass...
a) points south
b) tries to point downward
c) spins around and around

8 Where can you visit Big Ben?
a) Amsterdam   b) Barcelona   c) London

9 Who are the native people of Australia?
a) the Aborigines   b) the Eskimos   c) the Comanches

1. An Antarctic research station recorded the lowest temperature ever. What was it?
   a) −40°C (−40°F)
   b) −60°C (−75°F)
   c) −90°C (−130°F)

2. What's the largest country in Europe?
   a) Ukraine   b) France   c) Spain

3. What did Han Solo fly in *Star Wars*?
   a) Death Star
   b) TIE Fighter
   c) Millennium Falcon

4. Would you ever see a polar bear eating a penguin in the wild?

5 Which of these continents is entirely in the Northern Hemisphere?

a) Africa

b) Australia

c) Europe

6 'Smoke that Thunders' is the translation of the local name for the largest what in the world: volcano or waterfall?

7 The deepest part of the world's oceans is the Challenger Deep in the Mariana Trench. Which ocean is it in?

a) Atlantic

b) Indian

c) Pacific

8 Which of these is a real species of penguin you could find in Antarctica: Macaroni or Spaghetti?

9 In 1871, what did the journalist Henry Morton Stanley say when he finally tracked down the explorer David Livingstone in Africa?

a) I have crossed so many, many miles to find you.

b) Good sir, we meet at last!

c) Dr. Livingstone, I presume?

1) Until 1896 in Britain, anyone who went for a drive had to have a man walk in front of their vehicle waving a red flag. Was he a...

a) policeman?   b) soldier?   c) judge?

2) Which rocket took astronauts to the Moon for the first time?

a) Apollo 1   b) Apollo 11   c) Apollo 13

3) Where can you see the ruins of ancient Inca temples?

a) Asia   b) Europe   c) South America

4) What are the little filled rice rolls that you can eat at restaurants in Japan?

a) sushi
b) saki
c) kayu

5) In ancient times, on which island was the monstrous Minotaur said to be trapped in a maze?

a) Corsica   b) Sicily   c) Crete

6) How long would a passenger ship take to sail from New York to Southampton, England?

a) one day   b) one week   c) one month

7) Which fictional bear was found at a train station, and has a particular liking for English marmalade?

a) Yogi   b) Paddington   c) Baloo

8) Where would you go to swim in the Blue Lagoon, which is heated by a volcano?

a) Iceland   b) Ireland   c) Israel

1. **When Neil Armstrong stepped onto the Moon, he said: "That's one small step for man..."**
   a) one giant leap into the unknown
   b) one giant leap for the stars
   c) one giant leap for mankind

2. **What's said to have been hidden in the US military base, Area 51?**
   a) Russian spy plane   b) UFO   c) pterodactyl

3. **Where did the Yellow Brick Road lead to in *The Wizard of Oz*?**
   a) the Emerald City   b) Neverland   c) Hogwarts

4. **The faster you travel, the slower time goes.**
   True or false?

5 Where is Neuschwanstein Castle?
- a) Spain
- b) Germany
- c) France

6 What was on the island of Alcatraz?
- a) maximum-security prison
- b) hospital
- c) monastery

7 Which is the longest mountain range in the world?
- a) Andes
- b) Himalayas
- c) Rockies

8 Where is Rome the capital city?
- a) Turkey
- b) Romania
- c) Italy

1) If you went on safari to see giraffes, would you visit the north or south of Africa?

2) If you drilled a hole from London straight through the Earth, would you come out nearest...
a) Argentina?   b) New Zealand?   c) Russia?

3) Is it hot or cold at the Equator?

4) Which city is famous for its red double-decker buses?
a) London   b) Paris   c) New York

5) Are there planes that can take off on water?

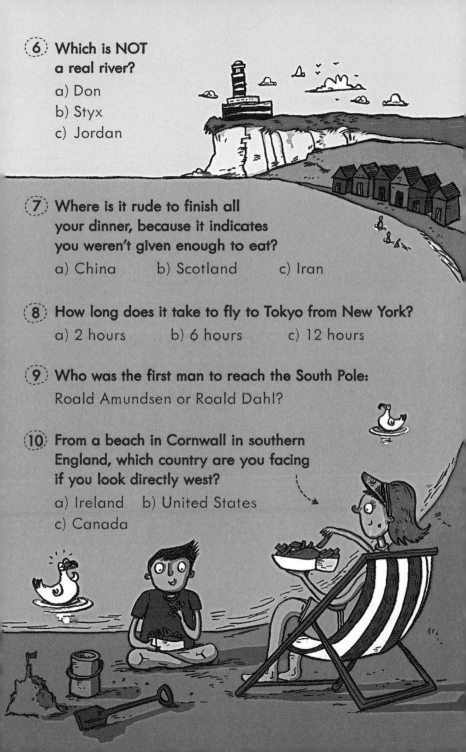

6 Which is NOT a real river?
   a) Don
   b) Styx
   c) Jordan

7 Where is it rude to finish all your dinner, because it indicates you weren't given enough to eat?
   a) China   b) Scotland   c) Iran

8 How long does it take to fly to Tokyo from New York?
   a) 2 hours   b) 6 hours   c) 12 hours

9 Who was the first man to reach the South Pole: Roald Amundsen or Roald Dahl?

10 From a beach in Cornwall in southern England, which country are you facing if you look directly west?
   a) Ireland   b) United States
   c) Canada

1. Which movie hero went to the ancient Middle Eastern city of Petra to find the Holy Grail?
   a) Indiana Jones
   b) Luke Skywalker
   c) Lara Croft

2. What is Australia's capital city?
   a) Sydney
   b) Melbourne
   c) Canberra

3. Where's the San Andreas Fault?
   a) Canada
   b) United States
   c) Mexico

4. Where can you spend roubles?
   a) Russia   b) India   c) Poland

5. Which is NOT a Mexican food?
   a) guacamole
   b) fajitas
   c) calamari

6 What's the station and platform number for the Hogwarts Express in the *Harry Potter* books?

a) Euston Station, Platform 4 1/2
b) Charing Cross Station, Platform 7 2/3
c) King's Cross Station, Platform 9 3/4

7 Which airline has a picture of a kangaroo on its planes?

a) British Airways   b) Qantas   c) Lufthansa

8 Which is the world's smallest country?

a) Monaco   b) Liechtenstein   c) Vatican City State

9 Where did Charles Darwin see lots of giant tortoises?

a) Galápagos Islands   b) Barbados   c) Seychelles

28

1. **Which is the world's largest country?**
   a) China
   b) Russia
   c) United States

2. **Where are the ruins of Ancient Egypt?**
   a) Africa
   b) Oceania
   c) South America

3. **What can you watch in Spain:** bullfights or gladiator fights?

4. **Which country is NOT in Europe?**
   a) Iran   b) Ukraine   c) Estonia

5. **What's this huge canyon in the United States called?**

(6) **If a sailing ship was caught in the doldrums, what would happen?**
   a) It would speed up dramatically
   b) It would come almost to a complete stop
   c) It would sink

(7) **Which of these animals could you NOT see in the forests of eastern Russia?**
   a) tigers   b) bears   c) gorillas   d) wolves

(8) **What's unusual about the Spanish national anthem:**
   it has no words or it has no music?

(9) **Where can you see gauchos herding their livestock?**
   a) South Africa
   b) Argentina
   c) Greece

1. In a book by C.S. Lewis, where did four children find an entrance to Narnia?
   a) at the bottom of a well
   b) in a hidden cave
   c) at the back of a wardrobe

2. Glaciers are found in...
   a) Yemen   b) Dubai   c) Norway

3. Where in London can you see waxwork replicas of famous people?
   a) Houses of Parliament
   b) Madame Tussauds
   c) Tower of London

4. What is a group of small islands called?
   a) archipelago
   b) estuary
   c) lagoon

FLIZABETH II

IA

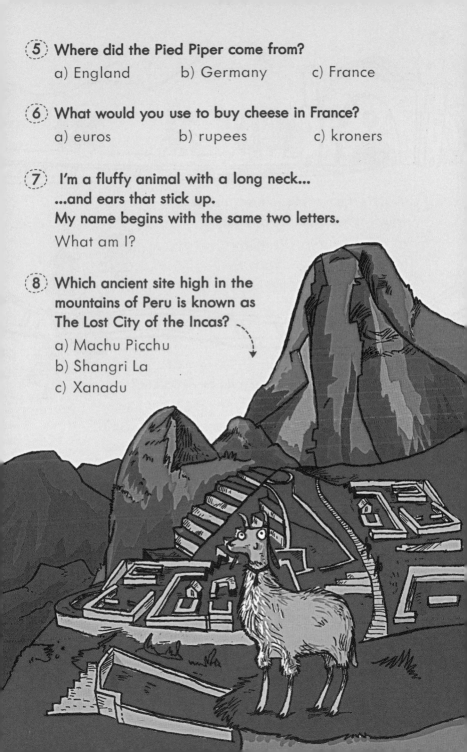

5 Where did the Pied Piper come from?

    a) England   b) Germany   c) France

6 What would you use to buy cheese in France?

    a) euros   b) rupees   c) kroners

7 I'm a fluffy animal with a long neck...
...and ears that stick up.
My name begins with the same two letters.
What am I?

8 Which ancient site high in the
mountains of Peru is known as
The Lost City of the Incas?

    a) Machu Picchu
    b) Shangri La
    c) Xanadu

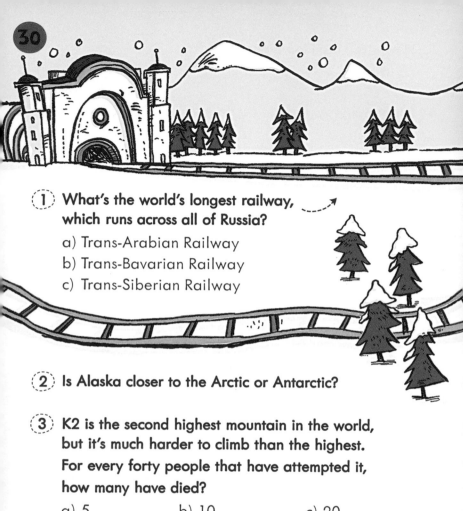

1) **What's the world's longest railway, which runs across all of Russia?**

a) Trans-Arabian Railway
b) Trans-Bavarian Railway
c) Trans-Siberian Railway

2) **Is Alaska closer to the Arctic or Antarctic?**

3) **K2 is the second highest mountain in the world, but it's much harder to climb than the highest. For every forty people that have attempted it, how many have died?**

a) 5   b) 10   c) 20

Владивосток

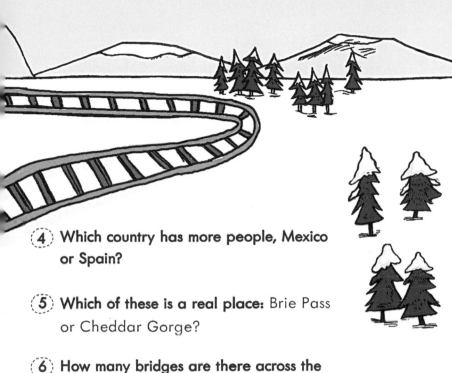

4. Which country has more people, Mexico or Spain?

5. Which of these is a real place: Brie Pass or Cheddar Gorge?

6. How many bridges are there across the Amazon river?

   a) none   b) over 200   c) over 400

7. Choose the word that completes this old saying: 'Sail the ... seas.'

   a) five   b) seven   c) nine

8. How much did the USA pay in 1867 to buy Alaska from Russia?

   a) $7.2 million   b) $72 million   c) $720 million

31

1. Which is closest to the South Pole?
   a) South Africa   b) Chile   c) New Zealand

2. Which city has the largest population in the world?
   a) Mexico City   b) London   c) Tokyo

3. In China, are dragons said to bring good or bad luck?

4. Is sangria a Spanish drink or a French drink?

5. The Orient Express train originally ran from Paris to where?
   a) Moscow   b) Istanbul   c) Kiev

6 Match each word for 'boat' with its language:

a) лодка   1) Greek

b) βάρκα   2) French

c) bateau   3) Russian

7 Eskimos have over 50 words for snow.

True or false?

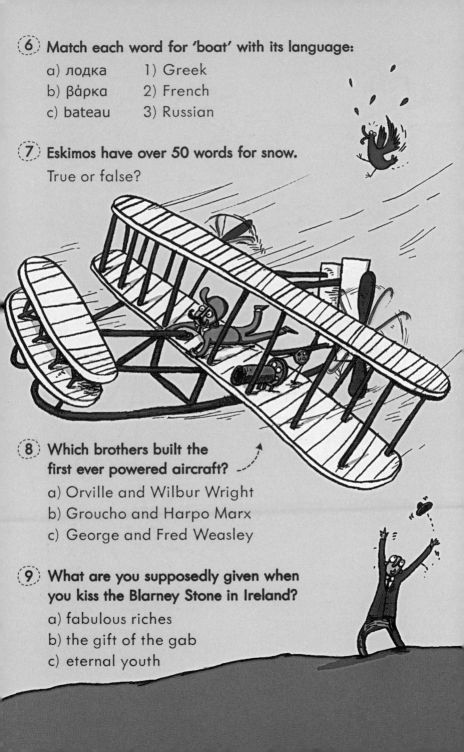

8 Which brothers built the first ever powered aircraft?

a) Orville and Wilbur Wright

b) Groucho and Harpo Marx

c) George and Fred Weasley

9 What are you supposedly given when you kiss the Blarney Stone in Ireland?

a) fabulous riches

b) the gift of the gab

c) eternal youth

1. **Where could you go swimming with dolphins?**
   a) Caribbean Sea   b) Baltic Sea   c) Red Sea

2. **For six months of the year the Poles are lit by constant sunlight. What happens for the next six months?**
   a) the constant sunlight continues
   b) there's no sunlight at all
   c) the Sun sets at night

3. **How many states are there in the USA?**
   a) 20   b) 50   c) 65

4. **The Taj Mahal in India is a giant tomb built by the emperor Shah Jahan for his...**
   a) mother   b) daughter   c) wife

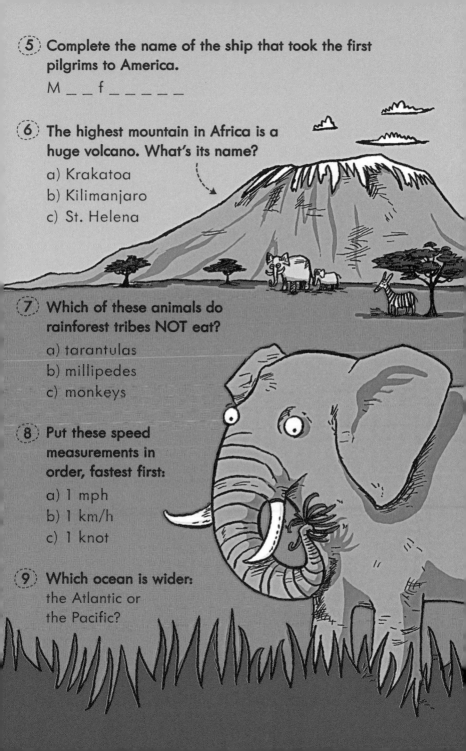

(5) Complete the name of the ship that took the first pilgrims to America.

M _ _ f _ _ _ _ _

(6) The highest mountain in Africa is a huge volcano. What's its name?

a) Krakatoa
b) Kilimanjaro
c) St. Helena

(7) Which of these animals do rainforest tribes NOT eat?

a) tarantulas
b) millipedes
c) monkeys

(8) Put these speed measurements in order, fastest first:

a) 1 mph
b) 1 km/h
c) 1 knot

(9) Which ocean is wider: the Atlantic or the Pacific?

1) What would you use to buy a curry dish in India?
   a) rupees   b) rubles   c) yen

2) Where can you see penguins in the wild?
   a) Canada
   b) Antarctica
   c) Finland

3) Which of these rivers is NOT in South America?
   a) Orinoco
   b) Limpopo
   c) Amazon

4) If you flew from Tokyo to London on New Year's Eve, would New Year come earlier or later than if you'd stayed in Japan?

5) Which loch (lake) in Scotland is said to hide an ancient monster?

a) Loch Lass   b) Loch Ness   c) Loch Bess

6) Is the driest place on Earth in the Sahara desert or Antarctica?

7) Every year, Mardi Gras festivals are held in New Orleans and other cities. What does 'Mardi Gras' mean?

a) Harvest Festival
b) Midsummer Dance
c) Fat Tuesday

8) Where do people traditionally dance flamenco?

a) Spain
b) Cuba
c) Georgia

1) **Which island is part of the Kingdom of Denmark, but is 50 times larger than Denmark itself?**

   a) Iceland   b) Ireland   c) Greenland

2) **Are most London taxis:**

   a) yellow?   b) black?   c) silver?

3) **If you were stranded on a desert island, which shape should you make on the beach to attract a search plane?**

   a) triangle   b) circle   c) square

4) **Where are the Pyramids of Giza?**

   a) Saudi Arabia   b) Egypt   c) Pakistan

5) Buñol in Spain has an unusual annual festival where people throw food at each other. Which type of food do they throw?

a) eggs   b) custard tarts   c) tomatoes

6) The speedy ships that sailed between Europe and China in the mid-nineteenth century were known as what?

a) coffee cutters
b) tea clippers
c) sugar sloops

7) What is the highest mountain in Western Europe?

a) Ben Nevis   b) Mont Blanc   c) Snowdon

8) What are the wild dogs in Australia called?

a) hyenas   b) dingoes   c) jackals

9) Which animal did the Ancient Egyptians believe was sacred?

a) owl   b) badger   c) cat

10) Alaska is the easternmost, westernmost and northernmost US state. Which is the southernmost?

a) Hawaii   b) Texas   c) Florida

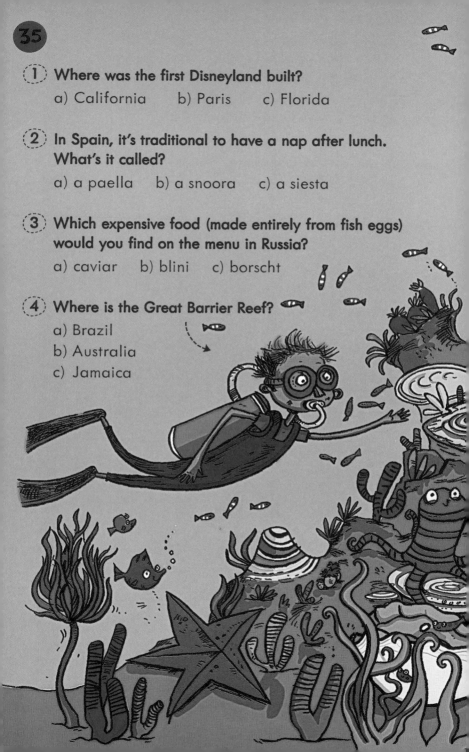

35

1 **Where was the first Disneyland built?**
   a) California   b) Paris   c) Florida

2 **In Spain, it's traditional to have a nap after lunch. What's it called?**
   a) a paella   b) a snoora   c) a siesta

3 **Which expensive food (made entirely from fish eggs) would you find on the menu in Russia?**
   a) caviar   b) blini   c) borscht

4 **Where is the Great Barrier Reef?**
   a) Brazil
   b) Australia
   c) Jamaica

5 What is the Swahili word for a journey?

a) trek   b) walkabout   c) safari

6 Why is Paris sometimes called the City of Light?

a) it was one of the first cities with gas streetlights

b) it gets a lot of sunshine all year round

c) it has an annual candle festival

7 Which country has the longest coastline in the world?

a) Norway

b) Russia

c) Canada

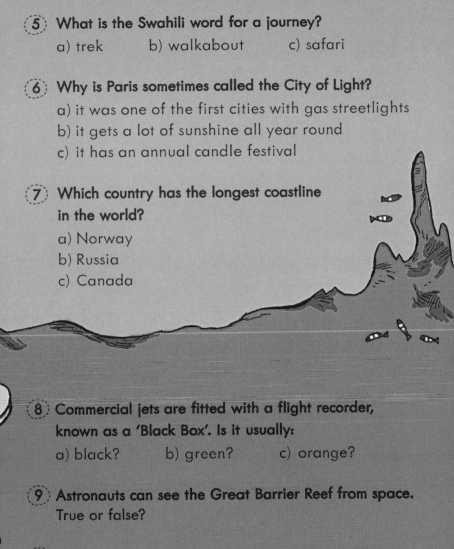

8 Commercial jets are fitted with a flight recorder, known as a 'Black Box'. Is it usually:

a) black?   b) green?   c) orange?

9 Astronauts can see the Great Barrier Reef from space. True or false?

10 Flying from London to New York across the Atlantic Ocean is known as 'Crossing the...?'

a) lake

b) pond

c) puddle

1. Seven countries in central Asia end in 'stan', Kazakhstan, Uzbekistan, Turkmenistan, Pakistan, Tajikistan, Kyrgyzstan... and what is the seventh?

2. Which can you see from the International Space Station: the Pyramids of Giza or the Great Wall of China?

3. When did the first person land on the Moon?
   a) 1928   b) 1969   c) 2001

4. What made the strange stone columns of the Giant's Causeway in Northern Ireland?
   a) volcanic eruption
   b) tidal wave
   c) hurricane

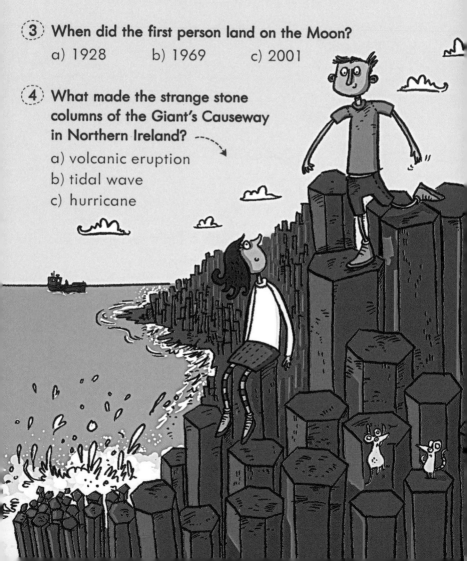

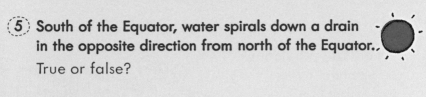

5. South of the Equator, water spirals down a drain in the opposite direction from north of the Equator. True or false?

6. Which is a popular beach in Sydney, Australia?
   a) Barbie Beach
   b) Bondi Beach
   c) Bonza beach

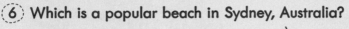

7. What's the longest river in the USA?
   a) Mississippi
   b) Hudson
   c) Rio Grande

8. According to legend, what's buried under Europe's largest volcano, Mount Etna, in Sicily?

   a) a huge, fire-breathing monster
   b) the gate to the underworld
   c) the philosopher's stone

1. Where can you ride an elephant up to the Amber Fort?
   a) Tashkent
   b) Jaipur
   c) Karachi

2. If you were cycling through Britain, which side of the road should you be on: right or left?

3. In a book by Mark Twain, which river did Tom Sawyer and Huckleberry Finn sail down?
   a) Colorado   b) Rio Grande   c) Mississippi

4. Roughly how many languages are there in the world?
   a) 70
   b) 700
   c) 7,000

5. Complete the name of the huge waterfall in North America that Charles Blondin crossed on stilts:

N _ _ g _ _ _   F _ _ _ _ _

6. What is borscht, the national dish of Ukraine?
   a) beetroot soup
   b) potato curry
   c) carrot cake

7. Rainforests grow near the:
   a) North Pole
   b) South Pole
   c) Equator

8. What's the Gulf Stream?
   a) a warm ocean current in the Atlantic
   b) a warm northerly wind from Africa
   c) a river in Hawaii that's heated by a volcano

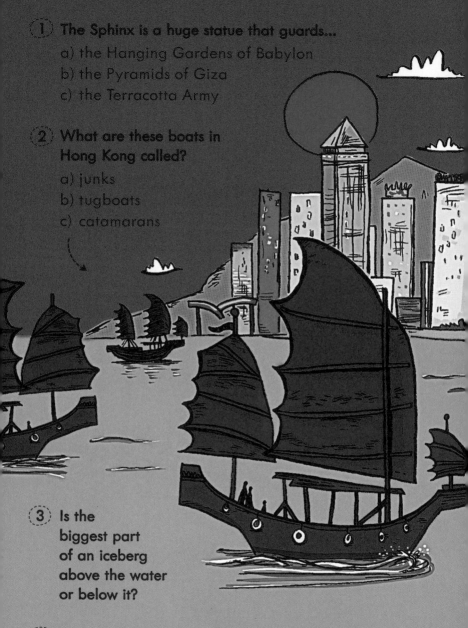

1) **The Sphinx is a huge statue that guards...**
   a) the Hanging Gardens of Babylon
   b) the Pyramids of Giza
   c) the Terracotta Army

2) **What are these boats in Hong Kong called?**
   a) junks
   b) tugboats
   c) catamarans

3) **Is the biggest part of an iceberg above the water or below it?**

4) **People travel to which island for its surfing beaches?**
   a) Ireland   b) Newfoundland   c) Hawaii

5. **What's the volcano near Tokyo in Japan called?**
   a) Mount Fuji   b) Mount Kodak   c) Mount Nikon

6. **What type of aircraft takes off vertically, and has rotors instead of wings?**
   a) hovercraft
   b) hang glider
   c) helicopter

7. **If you walk along Tower Bridge in London, which river are you crossing?**
   a) Severn   b) Mersey   c) Thames

8. **Where can you see people playing steel pans and wearing rasta hats?**
   a) Hawaii   b) Jamaica   c) Fiji

1 Where is Islamabad the capital city?
a) Iran   b) Pakistan   c) Bangladesh

2 Which river separates Mexico from the United States?
a) Rio Grande   b) Amazon   c) McKenzie

3 'Hakuna matata' is a Swahili phrase used in the movie *The Lion King*. What does it mean?
a) no worries   b) pardon me   c) I'll be back

4 You can go white-water rafting in river...
a) estuaries   b) deltas   c) rapids

5) If you're on the beach in Italy and someone says to you: "i tuoi piedi odorano di formaggio", what are they saying?

   a) The water is very warm.
   b) Your feet smell like cheese.
   c) You should put on some sunscreen.

6) Should ships at sea pass each other on the left or right?

7) Which country has borders with China, the United States, Finland and Ukraine?

   a) Canada
   b) Russia
   c) India

8) Where would you be if you saw these Maasai women?

   a) Kenya
   b) Argentina
   c) Japan

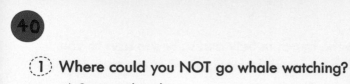

1 **Where could you NOT go whale watching?**
a) Switzerland
b) Canada
c) South Africa

2 **What is Japan's nickname?**
a) Land of the Rising Sun
b) Land of the Yellow Moon
c) Land of the Long Grass

3 **Where do one sixth of all the people in Africa live?**
a) Sierra Leone   b) Chad   c) Nigeria

4 **Complete this line from *The Rime of the Ancient Mariner*, a poem about a sailor adrift in the ocean:** 'Water, water everywhere, Nor any drop t _ d _ _ _ _ _.'

5 What word do Australians use for a 'dead river'?

  a) wallaby   b) boomerang   c) billabong

6 Lemurs are native to which island?

  a) Madagascar   b) Ireland   c) Greenland

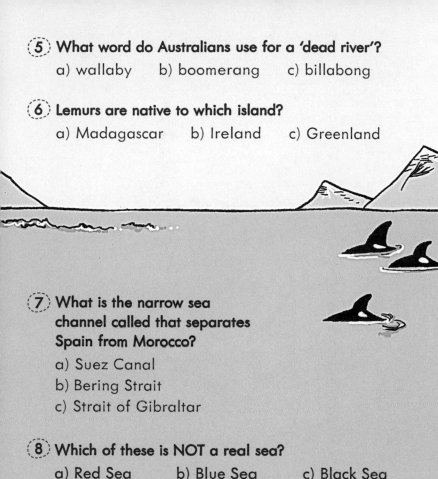

7 What is the narrow sea channel called that separates Spain from Morocco?

  a) Suez Canal
  b) Bering Strait
  c) Strait of Gibraltar

8 Which of these is NOT a real sea?

  a) Red Sea   b) Blue Sea   c) Black Sea

9 In 1789, there was a mutiny on board which ship as it was sailing across the Pacific Ocean?

  a) *HMS Bounty*
  b) *HMS Beagle*
  c) *HMS Victory*

10 What are mapmakers called?

  a) archaeologists
  b) cartographers
  c) geologists

1. Which character had a flying carpet?
   a) Ali Baba
   b) Sinbad
   c) Aladdin

2. Where are you more likely to be caught in an earthquake?
   a) San Francisco   b) New Delhi   c) Stockholm

3. Where can you see the ruins of ancient Aztec pyramids?
   a) Mexico   b) Canada   c) Vietnam

4. If you went down the West Coast of the United States, which place would you NOT go through?
   a) Los Angeles   b) New York   c) San Francisco

5 What type of boat is taking these people down the Mississippi river?

   a) tugboat

   b) rubber dinghy

   c) paddle steamer

6 When eating curry in India, which hand should you use?

   a) left   b) right

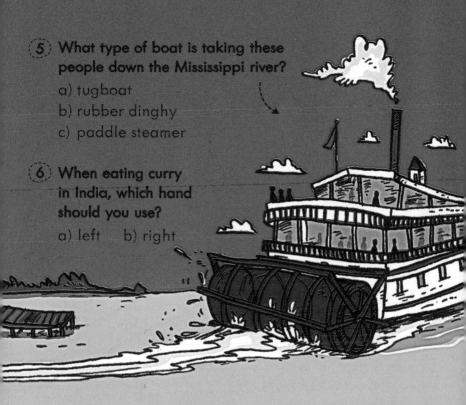

7 Where might you see a tiger in the wild?

   a) Asia   b) Africa   c) Europe

8 Where's the Sydney Opera House?

   a) England   b) Malaysia   c) Australia

9 On a desert trek, how long can a camel go without drinking?

   a) 4 months

   b) 4 weeks

   c) 4 days

42

1. Where can you see southern crowned pigeons and flame bowerbirds?
   a) England   b) Papua New Guinea   c) Mongolia

2. The flat-topped mountain overlooking Cape Town in South Africa is called...?
   a) Table Mountain
   b) Washboard Mountain
   c) Footstool Mountain

3. Which country's flag is nicknamed 'the star spangled banner'?
   a) United States   b) France   c) New Zealand

4. Which side of a ship is 'port,' left or right?

5) If a Frenchman walked into a glass door by mistake, what would he be most likely to say?

a) Je ne regrette rien!

b) Zut alors!

c) Merci!

6) Which European explorer ended up serving in the court of Kublai Khan in China?

a) Marco Polo

b) Hernán Cortés

c) Walter Raleigh

7) If you came across a rafflesia flower in Southeast Asia, what would it smell like?

a) Brussels sprouts

b) blue cheese

c) rotten meat

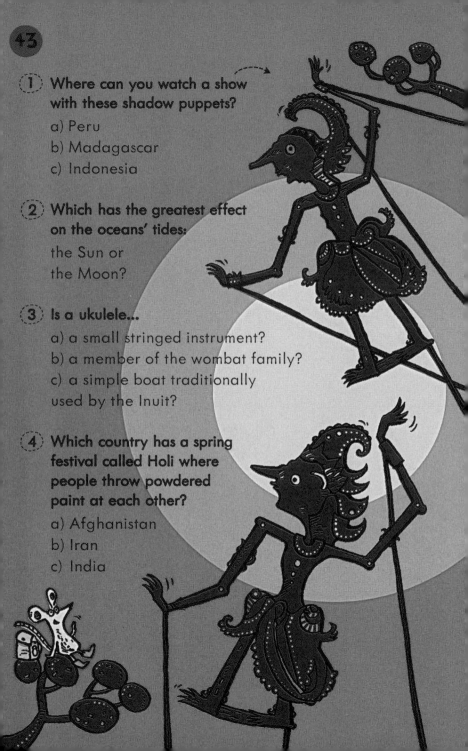

43

1) **Where can you watch a show with these shadow puppets?**
   a) Peru
   b) Madagascar
   c) Indonesia

2) **Which has the greatest effect on the oceans' tides:**
   the Sun or
   the Moon?

3) **Is a ukulele...**
   a) a small stringed instrument?
   b) a member of the wombat family?
   c) a simple boat traditionally used by the Inuit?

4) **Which country has a spring festival called Holi where people throw powdered paint at each other?**
   a) Afghanistan
   b) Iran
   c) India

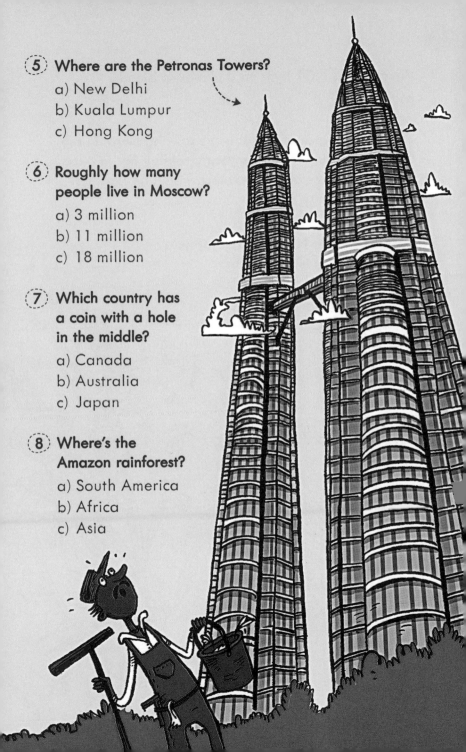

5 Where are the Petronas Towers?
  a) New Delhi
  b) Kuala Lumpur
  c) Hong Kong

6 Roughly how many people live in Moscow?
  a) 3 million
  b) 11 million
  c) 18 million

7 Which country has a coin with a hole in the middle?
  a) Canada
  b) Australia
  c) Japan

8 Where's the Amazon rainforest?
  a) South America
  b) Africa
  c) Asia

44

1. **Which city is NOT built on a cluster of islands?**
   a) Madrid   b) New York   c) Venice

2. **The wettest place on Earth is the town of Lloró, in the Colombian rainforest. If its yearly rainfall fell at once, how many floors of a towerblock would be flooded?**
   a) one   b) three   c) five

3. **Is Iceland in the Northern Hemisphere or the Southern Hemisphere?**

4. **What type of dancing can you see at the Rio Carnival in Brazil?**
   a) foxtrot
   b) tango
   c) samba

5 When it was completed in 1889, the Eiffel Tower was the tallest structure in the world.

True or false?

6 'Timbuktu' is the name for what?

a) a species of monkey
b) a type of mango
c) a town in Mali

7 Where does vodka come from?

a) Venezuela
b) Greece
c) Russia

8 Which river runs through Paris?

a) Seine
b) Danube
c) Tiber

9 Is it hot or cold in deserts at night?

45

1 What's the nickname for El Dorado, a mythical city buried deep in the Amazon rainforest?
a) Lost City of Gold
b) Lost City of Diamonds
c) Lost City of Chocolate

2 In ancient Greece and Rome, a coin was placed in dead people's mouths for the ferryman who carried their souls into the afterlife. Which river did they cross?
a) Euphrates   b) Styx   c) Mekong

3 Where is Kathmandu the capital city?
a) Senegal
b) Nepal
c) Peru

4 Where would you find a crow's nest: a hot-air balloon or a sailing ship?

5 The point on land that is furthest from the Earth's core is the top of Mount Everest. True or false?

6 What is the Amazon rainforest sometimes known as?
   a) the lungs of the world
   b) the heart of darkness
   c) the green goddess

7 Which of these is NOT a US state?
   a) New Mexico
   b) New Jersey
   c) New Brunswick

8 Which animals are the Canary Islands named after?
   a) cats   b) dogs   c) canaries

46

1. Which has more people:
   Brazil or Canada?

2. Where's Death Valley, the
   world's hottest desert?
   a) Australia
   b) Mexico
   c) United States

3. In Greek mythology, Icarus flew with wings
   made by his dad. Why did he plummet to his death?
   a) he panicked when he looked down
   b) the sun melted the wax holding his wings together
   c) he was attacked by the king of the birds

4. Complete the name of this Caribbean island:
   C _ _ _

5. Where is the largest active volcano in the world?
   a) Alaska   b) Portugal   c) Hawaii

6. Which language is spoken in the most countries?
   a) French
   b) Spanish
   c) English

7. Are all the oceans joined together?

8. Which direction on a map do lines of latitude go:

   north to south or east to west?

9. Where in Eastern Europe can you visit a 700 year-old salt mine with sculptures, chambers and an entire chapel carved out of salt?
   a) Greenland
   b) Finland
   c) Poland

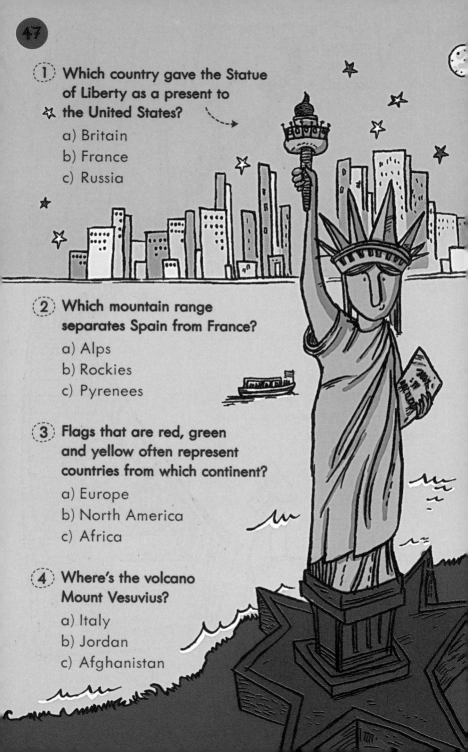

47

1) **Which country gave the Statue of Liberty as a present to the United States?**

a) Britain
b) France
c) Russia

2) **Which mountain range separates Spain from France?**

a) Alps
b) Rockies
c) Pyrenees

3) **Flags that are red, green and yellow often represent countries from which continent?**

a) Europe
b) North America
c) Africa

4) **Where's the volcano Mount Vesuvius?**

a) Italy
b) Jordan
c) Afghanistan

5) The Pharos of Alexandria was one of the ancient Seven Wonders of the World. What was it?
   a) a huge statue   b) a library   c) a lighthouse

6) Which word completes a nickname for any large city: 'The Big...?'
   a) Smoke   b) Fire   c) Steam

7) What was the original name of New York?
   a) New London   b) New Paris   c) New Amsterdam

8) The shortest commercial flight in the world lasts for less than two minutes. True or false?

9) Which country has the lowest birth rate in the world?
   a) Vatican City State   b) Russia   c) Norway

10) Stockholm is the capital city of which European country?
    a) Iceland
    b) Switzerland
    c) Sweden

48

1. Which ghost ship was said to be condemned to sail the seas for all eternity?
   a) *The Dawn Treader*
   b) *The Flying Dutchman*
   c) *The Golden Hind*

2. Which river runs through Rome?
   a) Euphrates
   b) Don
   c) Tiber

3. Where was the Terracotta Army sealed underground?
   a) Japan   b) China   c) Thailand

4. What's the nickname for an experienced old sailor:
   a spicy seacat or a salty seadog?

5) A marketplace in North Africa is called a...

a) bazaar   b) farrago   c) gumbo

6) Which city was built first?

a) Rome
b) Las Vegas
c) Sydney

7) What do climbers rub on their hands for extra grip?

a) olive oil
b) chalk
c) superglue

8) Who built Stonehenge?

a) ancient Egyptians
b) ancient Britons
c) ancient Greeks

9) Where do Inuit people live?

a) Africa
b) Australia
c) the Arctic

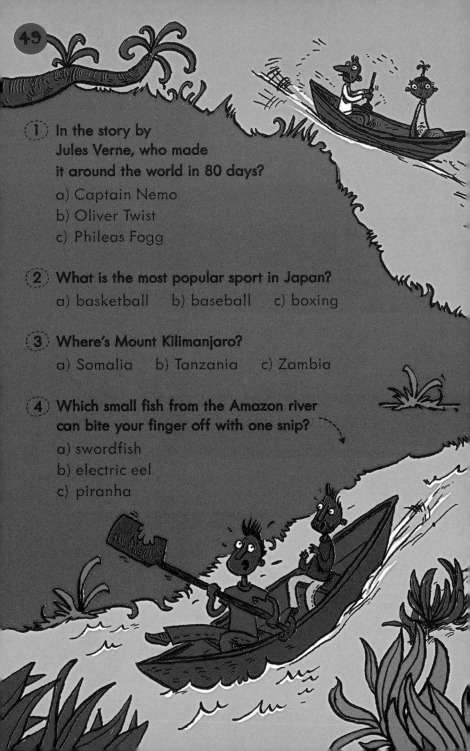

49

1) In the story by
Jules Verne, who made
it around the world in 80 days?
   a) Captain Nemo
   b) Oliver Twist
   c) Phileas Fogg

2) What is the most popular sport in Japan?
   a) basketball   b) baseball   c) boxing

3) Where's Mount Kilimanjaro?
   a) Somalia   b) Tanzania   c) Zambia

4) Which small fish from the Amazon river
can bite your finger off with one snip?
   a) swordfish
   b) electric eel
   c) piranha

5 Who led the first expedition to sail around the world, but died on the way?

a) Ferdinand Magellan
b) Christopher Columbus
c) Francis Drake

6 Where can you see lions in the wild?

a) South America   b) Africa   c) Oceania

7 What do you spend in Mexico?

a) pesos   b) dollars   c) dinars

8 In *Gulliver's Travels* by Jonathan Swift, which is the island where the people are no bigger than dolls?

a) Lillipick   b) Lilliput   c) Lollipot

50

1) Where can you watch the Highland Games?
   a) Scotland
   b) Sweden
   c) Netherlands

2) How far is it between Alaska in North America and Russia in Asia?
   a) 4km / 2.5 miles
   b) 400km / 250 miles
   c) 4,000km / 2,500 miles

3) Where would you find St. Paul's Cathedral?
   a) Dublin   b) Edinburgh   c) London

4) Do rivers flow to the sea or away from the sea?

5) **Who were the first people to reach the summit of Mount Everest?**
   a) Shackleton and Fiennes
   b) Hillary and Tenzing
   c) Morecambe and Wise

6) **Match the money symbol to the country where that currency is used:**
   a) €   1) Japan
   b) ¥   2) United States
   c) $ 3) Germany

7) **Long ago, these huge symbols were scored into the desert. They're called the Nazca Lines. Where are they?**
   a) Peru   b) Iraq   c) Namibia

1 **Where in England can you visit the house where William Shakespeare was born?**

a) Oxford   b) Portsmouth   c) Stratford-upon-Avon

2 Which is bigger, Canada or the United States?

3 Complete the directions that Peter Pan gives to Neverland: "Second star to the right, and..."

a) a left at the lights.

b) a hop, a skip and a jump.

c) straight on till morning.

4 What can you spend in Argentina?

a) pesos   b) rupees   c) pounds

5 Where's the Sahara desert?

a) Australia   b) Africa   c) North America

6 Who discovered the wreck of *Titanic* in 1985:
James Cameron or Robert Ballard?

7 Which country attracts the most tourists each year?
a) United States   b) France   c) Greece

8 The Spanish Steps are NOT in Spain.
True or false?

9 In *The Lord of the Rings* by J. R. R. Tolkien, where
were the hobbits Frodo and Sam trying to get to?
a) Mordor   b) Isengard   c) Middle Earth

10 Which Italian river completes a phrase that means
you've passed a point of no return? 'Crossing the...?'
a) Tiber   b) Rubicon   c) Po

11 According to the saying, where do all roads lead:
home or Rome?

12 What were the Hawaiian Islands originally known as?
a) Sandwich Islands
b) Pancake Islands
c) Taco Islands

Answers

1 **1.** a **2.** a **3.** b **4.** Jolly Roger **5.** b **6.** southeast **7.** yes (cobras are the snakes that are usually used) **8.** gondola

2 **1.** c **2.** a **3.** true **4.** b **5.** b (in *James and the Giant Peach*, by Roald Dahl) **6.** b **7.** a **8.** c **9.** c (there isn't any water on the Moon's surface, but early astronomers mistook the Moon's darker patches for seas, hence the name) **10.** b **11.** Davy Jones's Locker

3 **1.** a **2.** c **3.** b **4.** c **5.** a (it's a sea and the other two are oceans) **6.** c **7.** a **8.** b **9.** a **10.** c (Transylvania is an area of Romania, in Eastern Europe. Vlad the Impaler (nicknamed Dracula) had a blood-soaked reign there in the 15th century. Zanzibar is a group of islands off the coast of Tanzania that used to be a haunt for slave traders and pirates. Valhalla is a mythical hall for Viking warriors who died in battle.)

4 **1.** a (its first manned flight was in 1783) **2.** b (a desert is somewhere where it hardly ever rains or snows, and Antarctica is the most cloudless place on Earth) **3.** a **4.** c **5.** a **6.** a **7.** Mounties **8.** c **9.** b (the lake is so huge it contains 20% of the world's fresh water)

5 **1.** b **2.** a **3.** c **4.** b (Tokyo is a city; the other two are countries) **5.** a **6.** b **7.** b, a, c **8.** b **9.** front

6 **1.** yes (a passenger jet is struck by lightning about once a year, but is designed to withstand the strike) **2.** dawn and dusk (when it's cooler) **3.** c **4.** a **5.** a **6.** b **7.** a **8.** c **9.** c

7 1. c 2. a 3. c 4. b 5. Great Wall of China 6. b
(he was Pharaoh of Ancient Egypt from 1333-1323BC)
7. b (Montreal is a mainly French-speaking city) 8. b

8 1. Turkey 2. a 3. c 4. light (light travels at
1,079,252,849km/h (670,616,629mph), sound travels at
1,236km/h (768mph)) 5. c 6. Eiffel Tower 7. b 8. a 9. a

9 1. South (the North Pole is solid ice) 2. *Titanic* 3. b
4. a (sidewinding is the easiest way for a snake to move
across sand) 5. back (On a map of the world, time goes
forward as you move eastward. At the furthest point east
you reach the international date line. You are 24 hours
ahead of the furthest point west, but because the Earth is
round, if you take one more step, you go back 24 hours.)
6. the Northern Lights (they are also known as the Aurora
Borealis) 7. sea (roughly 70% of the Earth's surface is
covered by water) 8. c 9. c

10 1. a 2. b (they're the same units that boat speed is
measured in) 3. c 4. a 5. c (it's in Somalia, Africa) 6. b
(in the wild, pandas only live in China) 7. a 8. b

11 1. b 2. beaver 3. a 4. yes 5. a 6. c 7. Ayers Rock 8. a

12 1. a 2. a globe (Because the Earth isn't flat, drawing a
map of the world on a piece of paper distorts the size of
the countries.) 3. c 4. b 5. a 6. a 7. right 8. c

13 1. c 2. b (it's called the Sagrada Família and is famous for its strange stonework, which seems to have grown from the ground like a living thing) 3. false (And anyway, there's no point. Once they've gone past halfway, they might as well have set out in the opposite direction.) 4. a (it's so hot that virtually nothing can live there) 5. b 6. a2, b3, c1 7. West Coast 8. b 9. b

14 1. a 2. b (Lenin was the leader of the Russian Revolution in 1917) 3. England and France 4. New York 5. c 6. a 7. b 8. b

15 1. c (the writing on the signs is Japanese and Tokyo is famous for its neon lights) 2. a 3. false (it's ice hockey) 4. c 5. b 6. c (tigers live in Asia) 7. c 8. Mississippi 9. a 10. b

16 1. yes (they're vicious, cat-sized mammals) 2. c 3. b 4. b 5. b 6. b 7. a deep-sea submersible 8. true (it is in a special capital district so that no state is at an advantage by having the capital within its borders) 9. c 10. b

17 1. a 2. b 3. c 4. b 5. a (it set off from Southampton, England on April 10, 1912 and sank on April 15, two days' sail from New York) 6. a 7. Mount Olympus 8. b

18 1. mirage 2. c 3. c 4. a 5. c (the Dead Sea is so thick with salt it can support a person's weight) 6. a 7. c (this includes one stop – a direct flight means you don't change planes even if it lands for fuel) 8. a (chai means 'tea' in India)

19 **1.** a **2.** The seven continents are: Africa, Antarctica, Asia, Europe, North America, Oceania and South America. **3.** a **4.** c (there's a star for every American state) **5.** b (he was from the former Soviet Union, and blasted into space on April 12, 1961) **6.** a **7.** c **8.** b

20 **1.** b **2.** b **3.** South Pole (The South Pole is in Antarctica, which is the highest continent in the world because the ground is covered by a sheet of ice so thick it swallows up mountains. It's this extra height that makes the South Pole colder than the North Pole.) **4.** c (Russia is so vast that while the sun is rising on one side of the country, it's setting on the other) **5.** b **6.** c **7.** c **8.** b

21 **1.** b **2.** c **3.** b (at the Poles in winter the Sun never rises) **4.** North Pole **5.** b **6.** a **7.** b, a, c **8.** a

22 **1.** My bull has escaped! **2.** b **3.** Grandfather Frost **4.** c **5.** pirates **6.** b (it's pronounced (roughly): Thlan-vire-poolth-gwin-gill-go-ger-u-queern-drob-oollth-thland-us-ill-eeo-go-go-goc-h) **7.** b (the Magnetic pole is under your feet. This is the Pole that compasses point toward. It's near the famous geographic North Pole, but moves slightly each year.) **8.** c **9.** a

23 **1.** c (it was recorded in 1983 at a Russian station called Vostok) **2.** a (Russia doesn't count because only part of it is in Europe) **3.** c **4.** no (polar bears live in the Arctic, and penguins in the Antarctic) **5.** c **6.** waterfall (It is the locals' name for Victoria Falls in Africa. Although it is neither the highest nor the widest, it is the largest single sheet of falling water in the world.) **7.** c **8.** Macaroni **9.** c

24 1. a 2. b 3. c 4. a 5. c 6. b 7. b 8. a

25 1. c 2. b (it's said to have crash-landed in Roswell, New Mexico, and been taken to Area 51 in Nevada) 3. a 4. true (Here's an example: Neil and Buzz are 25 years old. Neil flies in a rocket to the nearest star to the Sun, at half the speed of light. Buzz stays on Earth. When Neil returns he is 66 years old. Buzz is 72.) 5. b 6. a 7. a 8. c

26 1. south 2. b (you'd come out in the ocean – 1,000km / 600 miles southeast of New Zealand) 3. hot 4. a 5. yes (they're called seaplanes) 6. b 7. a 8. c 9. Roald Amundsen (Roald Dahl was named after him) 10. c

27 1. a (Petra was called the 'Temple of the Sun' in the film) 2. c 3. b (the San Andreas Fault is a place where two plates of rocky ground are sliding past each other (very, very slowly), which causes earthquakes) 4. a 5. c 6. c 7. b 8. c (The Vatican is where the Pope lives. It's an area in the middle of Italy's capital city (Rome) but is not controlled by the Italian government.) 9. a

28 1. b 2. a 3. bullfights 4. a 5. the Grand Canyon 6. b (The doldrums are areas of low pressure around the Equator where the prevailing winds are very calm.) 7. c 8. it has no words 9. b

29 1. c (from *The Lion, the Witch and the Wardrobe*) 2. c 3. b 4. a 5. b 6. a 7. llama 8. a

30 1. c 2. Arctic 3. b 4. Mexico 5. Cheddar Gorge (it's near the English village of Cheddar, in Somerset) 6. a (Although the Amazon is one of the longest rivers in the world, it flows through dense rainforest where there are very few roads and cities, and it can usually be crossed by ferry.) 7. b 8. a (At the time, Alaska was considered an icy wasteland, and many Americans actually thought that they had paid too much.)

31 1. b 2. c 3. good luck 4. Spanish 5. b 6. a3, b1, c2 7. false (Eskimo has about the same number of words for snow as English. But the Sami people, who live in the far North of the Nordic countries, have about 300 words for snow.) 8. a (the first flight took place in 1903) 9. b

32 1. a 2. b (While one Pole is in constant sunlight the other is in constant darkness. The Earth is tilted toward the Sun, so as one Pole faces the Sun the other faces away.) 3. b 4. c 5. *Mayflower* 6. b 7. b (many millipedes are poisonous) 8. c, a, b 9. Pacific

33 1. a 2. b 3. b (it's in Africa) 4. earlier (see note for answer 5 in quiz 9) 5. b 6. Antarctica (the McMurdo Dry Valleys are considered to be the place on Earth most similar to the surface of Mars) 7. c 8. a

34 1. c 2. b 3. a (a triangle is an international distress symbol) 4. b 5. c (the festival is called La Tomatina) 6. b 7. b 8. b 9. c (they were prized in society for controlling vermin) 10. a

35 1. a 2. c 3. a 4. b 5. c 6. a 7. c (Although Russia is larger, Canada's overall coastline is longer because it has so many islands.) 8. c (the orange makes it stand out if it needs to be retrieved from wreckage) 9. true 10. b

36 **1.** Afghanistan **2.** the Pyramids of Giza (The Pyramids are quite easy to spot because they're wide and cast big shadows. The Great Wall of China is virtually impossible to see from space because it's thin and blends in with the surrounding ground.) **3.** b **4.** a **5.** false (anywhere in the world, water can spiral down a drain in either direction) **6.** b **7.** a **8.** a

37 **1.** b (also called Amer Fort, it's about 10km (6 miles) from the city, in the north of India) **2.** left **3.** c **4.** c **5.** Niagara Falls (he also crossed it in many other ways, including blindfolded, carrying his manager on his back, and once he even sat down in the middle to cook an omelette) **6.** a **7.** c **8.** a

38 **1.** b **2.** a **3.** below it (icebergs are floating in the sea, only the top part sticks out above the water) **4.** c **5.** a **6.** c **7.** c **8.** b

39 **1.** b **2.** a **3.** a **4.** c **5.** b **6.** left **7.** b **8.** a

40 **1.** a (Switzerland has no coastline) **2.** a **3.** c **4.** to drink **5.** c **6.** a **7.** c **8.** b **9.** a **10.** b

41 **1.** c **2.** a **3.** a **4.** b (New York is on the East Coast) **5.** c **6.** b (The left hand is only used to serve food onto your plate. The right hand is kept clean for scooping up your food with flat breads.) **7.** a **8.** c **9.** b

42 **1.** b **2.** a **3.** a **4.** left **5.** b **6.** a **7.** c (its nickname is 'corpse flower')

43 **1.** c **2.** Moon **3.** a **4.** c **5.** b **6.** b **7.** c **8.** a

44 1. a 2. b 3. Northern Hemisphere 4. c 5. true 6. c
7. c 8. a 9. cold (deserts tend to be cold at night because
there's no moisture in the air, or clouds in the sky, to stop
the heat from escaping)

45 1. a (In Spanish, el dorado means 'golden one'. There was
a local tribe whose kings used to cover themselves in gold
dust, then sail out into a sacred lake to offer treasures to
their goddess. The legend grew from this, and local people
would get rid of European explorers by saying the lost city
of gold was "over there" in the distance.) 2. b 3. b
4. a sailing ship 5. false (the Earth bulges at the Equator,
so although the top of Mount Everest is the highest point
above sea level, the top of Mount Chimborazo in Ecuador
is further away from the Earth's core.) 6. a (the plantlife
there provides over 20% of the planet's oxygen) 7. c (it's a
Canadian province) 8. b (The name most likely comes from
the Latin name *canariae insulae*, meaning 'island of the
dogs'. Canaries are named after the islands, not the other
way around.)

46 1. Brazil 2. c (its record temperature is 56.7°C (134°F))
3. b 4. Cuba 5. c (it's called Mauna Loa) 6. c 7. yes
8. east to west 9. c (the tunnels are over 300km / 200
miles long (although the tourist route is 3.5km (2.2 miles)),
and there's also an underground lake)

47 1. b (the statue was built in France and transported to
America in 1885) 2. c 3. c 4. a 5. c 6. a 7. c (it was
originally a Dutch settlement, but was renamed after the
Duke of York when English forces seized control of it)
8. true (it is between Westray and Papa Westray in the
Orkney Islands) 9. a (Housing the head of the Catholic
Church, it has an official birth rate of zero.) 10. c

48 **1.** b **2.** c **3.** b (thousands of soldiers made from terracotta clay were buried alongside China's first emperor, Qin Shihuang, to guard him in the afterlife) **4.** salty seadog **5.** a **6.** a **7.** b **8.** b **9.** c

49 **1.** c **2.** b **3.** b **4.** c **5.** a (he died in the Philippines in 1521, about two thirds of the way through his 'round the world' voyage) **6.** b **7.** a **8.** b

50 **1.** a **2.** a (the far east of Russia nearly reaches the western tip of Alaska) **3.** c **4.** to the sea **5.** b **6.** a3, b1, c2 **7.** a

51 **1.** c **2.** Canada **3.** c (That's the line from the Disney film. In the original play it's "second to the right and then straight on till morning".) **4.** a **5.** b **6.** Robert Ballard (James Cameron directed the 1997 film *Titanic*) **7.** b (France regularly receives over 80 million visitors each year) **8.** true (they are in Rome, Italy) **9.** a **10.** b (It marked the point where Roman generals had to disband their armies before re-entering Italy. Not doing this was punishable by death. In 49 BC, Julius Caesar crossed it with his army, effectively declaring civil war on the Roman Senate.) **11.** Rome **12.** a (Captain Cook named the islands after the Earl of Sandwich)

With thanks to Michael Hill

First published in 2015 by Usborne Publishing Ltd, 83–85 Saffron Hill, London ECIN 8RT, England.